THE DAWN OF CANADA

Douglas Baldwin

Weigl
CALGARY
www.weigl.com

We acknowledge the financial support of the Government of Canada through the Book Publishing Industry Development Program (BPIDP) for our publishing activities.

Published by Weigl Educational Publishers Limited
6325 – 10 Street SE
Calgary, Alberta, Canada
T2H 2Z9

Web site: www.weigl.com

Copyright ©2003 WEIGL EDUCATIONAL PUBLISHERS LIMITED

All rights reserved. No part of this publication may be reproduced, stored in a retrieval system, or transmitted in any form or by any means, electronic, mechanical, photocopying, recording, or otherwise, without the prior written permission of the publisher.

National Library of Canada Cataloguing-in-Publication Data

Baldwin, Douglas, 1944-
 The Dawn of Canada/ Douglas Baldwin.

(Canadian history)
Includes bibliographical references and index.
For use in grades 6-8.
ISBN 1-55388-010-2

 1. Canada--Discovery and exploration--Juvenile literature. 2. Native peoples--Canada--Juvenile literature. I. Title. II. Series: Canadian history (Calgary, Alta.)

FC300.B34 2002   971   C2002-901452-2   E101.B34 2002

Printed in the United States of America
1 2 3 4 5 6 7 8 9 0   06 05 04 03 02

Project Coordinator
Michael Lowry
Editor
Lynn Hamilton
Copy Editor
Diana Marshall
Photo Researcher
Nicole Bezic King
Daorcey Le Bray
Designer
Warren Clark
Layout
Bryan Pezzi

Credits
Every reasonable effort has been made to trace ownership and to obtain permission to reprint copyright material. The publishers would be pleased to have any errors or omissions brought to their attention so that they may be corrected in subsequent printings.

Cover: Rice Gatherers (Architect of the Capitol/34115); Cabot (Courtesy Rogers Communications Inc.); **Architect of the Capitol:** page 9; **Bettman/CORBIS/MAGMA:** page 29; **Bob Krist/CORBIS/MAGMA:** page 28; **©The British Museum:** pages 6, 33; **Glenbow Archives:** pages 12 (NA-674-7), 13 (NA-141-4), 14 (NA-1700-141); **Kerr Historical Atlas TNS 1975:** page 24; **Metropolitan Museum of Art, Gift of J. Pierpont Morgan, 1900 (00.18.2):** page 25; **Museum of Civilization (K78-148):** page 17; **National Archives of Canada:** pages 3 top (A.M. Fink/C-2263), 3 middle (H. Holland/C-11413), 3 bottom (A.J. Miller/C-403), 7 (A.M. Fink/C-2263), 8 (P. Rindisbacher/C-1917), 10 (W.W. Wrathall/PA-95509), 11 (Joanna S. Wilson/C-74693), 15 (A.J. Miller/C-403), 22 (J. Walker/C-5539), 23 (NMC 27654), 30 (Pierre Desceliers/NMC 40461), 31 (H.R. Perrigard/C-12235), 32 (H. Holland/C-11413), 34 (C-13320), 35 (C.W. Jefferys/C-98232), 36 (C-17727), 37 (J. Collier/C-002061), 41L (C-38862), 41R (N. Shanawdithit/C-28544); **©National Gallery of Canada:** page 43; **National Library of Canada:** pages 5, 40; **Prentice-Hall of Canada Ltd:** page 27; **Courtesy Rogers Communications Inc.:** pages 21, 26; **Toronto Public Library:** page 16.

CONTENTS

The First Peoples 4

Fishers and Hunters of the Arctic 6

Hunters of the Western Subarctic 7

Hunters of the Eastern Subarctic 8

Fishers of the Northwest Coast 10

Fishers and Hunters of the Interior Plateau 12

Bison Hunters of the Plains 14

Farmers of the Northeastern Woodlands 16

Canada's First Peoples 18

Arrival of the Vikings 20

The Vikings Meet the Skraelings 22

An Age of Discovery 23

Columbus Sets Sail 24

Cabot Rediscovers Canada 26

The Portuguese Explore North America 28

Giovanni da Verrazzano 29

Cartier's Voyages of Exploration 30

The Search for the Northwest Passage 32

Champlain in New France 34

Henry Hudson 36

European Explorers in North America 38

The Beothuks of Newfoundland 40

A Meeting of Cultures 42

Quiz 44

Conclusion/Further Information 46

Glossary 47

Index 48

The First PEOPLES

Aboriginal peoples believe that they originated in North America when the land and their people were created long ago.

People lived in North America for thousands of years before European explorers first approached its shores. Groups of Aboriginal peoples lived all over the continent. Aboriginal peoples believe that they originated in North America when the land and their people were created long ago. Each Aboriginal group has its own unique creation story.

Scientists have developed their own theories about where the ancestors of Canada's Aboriginal peoples may have originated. These ideas are based on clues found by scientists. Similar pieces of bones, stone tools, and weapons have been found at archaeological sites in northeastern Asia and northwestern Canada. This has led many scientists to believe that Aboriginal groups emigrated from Asia about 14,000 years ago, when a land bridge joined Siberia and present-day Alaska. Some archaeologists believe the Aboriginal peoples used this bridge to walk across to North America. According to the theory, they then moved south, following an ice-free opening in the glaciers. Over the years, they migrated throughout North and South America following game. Other scientists speculate that people may have crossed the oceans on boats from Australia and Europe, and may have arrived much earlier than previously thought.

Canada is a large country with several geographic regions. Each region differs from the others by the land, plants, climate, and resources in the area. The first peoples who lived in the different regions adapted lifestyles that suited the climates and resources. Sometimes, groups shared a common language or way of life. Most groups had their own ways of life, spiritual beliefs, and methods of keeping order. They had well-developed political, social, and economic systems, as well as numerous languages and dialects as different from each other as English is from Chinese. Although children learned skills that were specific to their lifestyle, the methods of education were similar among the many Aboriginal groups. Children learned the ways of their people by observing experts and elders, and by listening to their tales, myths, and oral histories.

FURTHER UNDERSTANDING

Archaeological sites Artifacts are the objects and remains of peoples from ancient times. Archaeologists look for places, or sites, where they may find clues about peoples from the past. When stones found at sites in Canada were not of the type normally found in that area, some scientists concluded that the people who lived there had traded for the stones or travelled long distances to get them. Other scientists have examined the oldest skeletal remains found in America. They question whether the first peoples were really all of Asian descent, since some human remains show African, European, Australian, or Polynesian traits. New clues allow scientists to reconsider their theories about the origins Canada's first peoples.

Oral histories Few written records exist on the ancestors of Aboriginal peoples. Scientists learn about their lives from artifacts and from oral stories. Oral histories are stories repeated many times as they are passed on from person to person, and from generation to generation. To share accurate oral histories, individuals must be careful not to change the meaning. Interpreting stories and myths requires care. The characters in myths and stories of the Aboriginal peoples often teach lessons using statements that are not intended to be true. It is necessary to understand the culture and language to understand the deeper meanings.

How the Good Spirits Came to Rule the World

This Huron story is about how the world was created.

"Long, long ago, there was nothing but water everywhere. The only living beings were the water animals and birds.

In a spirit world far above the skies lived Sky-Man and Sky-Woman. One day, Sky-Man became very ill. Sky-Woman, who was going to have a baby, went into the forest to get some medicine plants. As she dug around the roots of a tree, she broke a hole in the sky.

Down, down she fell through this bottomless hole toward the water. Two loons flying over the water looked up. They could see Sky-Woman falling. Spreading their wide wings, the loons caught Sky-Woman and gently carried her down toward the sea below. While they carried her, the loons cried out for help to the other water creatures.

All the water animals rushed together as soon as they heard the loons call. Great Turtle ordered the creatures to swim to the bottom of the sea. One by one, each animal brought up some earth and piled it on top of Great Turtle's back.

Just in time, Great Turtle swam over to catch Sky-Woman. The loons dropped her on the soft earth piled on his back.

Sky-Woman spread the earth all over Great Turtle's shell to make dry land. The land continued to spread. Soon, plants began to grow.

Sky-Woman built herself a house under a large tree. She waited for her baby to be born.

Surprise! Sky-Woman had twin sons, but she did not live to see them grow. She died and was buried in the earth. Her last gifts to the world were three special plants. Corn, beans, and squash grew from her body. Later, people learned how to harvest these foods and to gather seeds for planting."

■ *Baggattaway* was an early form of lacrosse, popular among the Iroquois. The Iroquois lived in Canada's Northeastern Woodlands.

Fishers and Hunters of the ARCTIC

Several Inuit inventions are admired today, such as the igloo and the kayak.

Life was not easy in the Far North—the Arctic region. Since it was challenging to live in the Arctic, the peoples of the area, the Inuit, faced little competition from other groups. The region has long, cold, harsh winters and short summers. In the middle of winter, there is a period when the Sun never rises. While there are no trees in the Arctic, there are some shrubs that grow berries in summer. The Inuit relied mainly on fishing and hunting for their dietary needs.

Inuit groups communicated using many dialects, but their language base was Inuktitut. The size of the Inuit groups varied with the seasons. In summer, people lived in small family hunting groups. Some hunted caribou or moved to the coast to fish and gather shellfish and berries. In winter, Inuit peoples relied on stored food and the results of seal hunts. For winter hunts, they gathered in large groups, and many hunters worked together.

For the Inuit, the family was the most important social unit, and marriage was a necessary part of survival in the Arctic. Both the husbands and the wives had their own tools, goods, and possessions. The men were responsible for building the houses, hunting, and fishing, while the women took care of cooking, dressing of animal skins, and making clothing.

The Inuit are known for their creative methods of adapting to their environment. Several of their inventions are admired today, such as their domed snowhouse, the igloo. The kayak, the Inuit's principal means of water transportation, is another innovative invention. The Inuit relied on sleds pulled by dog teams for transportation over land.

■ In order to survive in the Arctic, the Inuit we warm, protective clothing made from the skins caribou, polar bears, seals, or walruses.

FURTHER UNDERSTANDING

Igloo Some Inuit peoples in the Arctic lived in snowhouses for most of the year. These igloos could be big enough for two or more families. They were about 3 metres high and 4 metres across. Other igloos were smaller, temporary shelters used when hunting or travelling. Using shovels and knives made of wood or bone, the Inuit cut blocks of hard snow or ice. They stacked the blocks upward to form a dome. Passages were built for entrances. The floor of the entry was lower than the floor inside the house. This helped keep warm air inside and cold air outside.

Seal hunts In winter, Inuit hunters waited at seals' breathing holes in the ice. When a seal came to the surface for air, the hunter killed it with a harpoon. Harpoons had a stone or iron point attached to a pole by a sealskin line. Inuit hunters also waited for seals to climb out onto the ice. Sometimes, they imitated the movements of the seals to avoid scaring the seals. Seals were also hunted in the water from kayaks.

The Dawn of Canada

Hunters of the Western SUBARCTIC

The people of the Subarctic inhabited the largest area of all the Aboriginal peoples. The Western Subarctic stretches from the western Hudson Bay area to nearly the Bering Sea. Peoples of the Western Subarctic, including the Dene, or Chipewyans, and the Yellowknives, belong to the Athapaskan language base.

Food is not plentiful in the western belt of forest between Alaska and Hudson Bay. The soil is poor, except in the Mackenzie Valley. The weather is bitterly cold for most of the year. During winter, freezing winds from the Arctic stunts the growth of trees and keeps the ground permanently frozen. Wintering herds of caribou feed on moss and **lichens**, and find shelter in groves of small trees and bushes.

The Chipewyans and the Yellowknives lived along the edge of this northern forest. During winter, they stayed in the trees. In summer, they hunted the caribou on the open tundra plains. The Beavers, or Dunne-za, who lived to the southwest, were named after the animal they depended on for their survival. The Kutchin lived farther north than any other Subartic group.

Reliance on the caribou, which is a migratory animal, meant that food supplies were irregular. To avoid famine, reserve supplies of food were **cached** for use when food was scarce. Meat was frozen, fried, or made into pemmican.

For most people in this area, furnishings were mainly caribou or bearskins spread on the ground, with a layer of spruce boughs laid underneath for sleeping. Since related families travelled together in small bands to hunt caribou and other animals, shelter and furnishings had to be portable. In winter, snowshoes were used to travel over deep snow, and loads were placed on toboggans. Summer travel was mainly done on foot or by canoe. While their leaders were experienced hunters, they had little authority over the group members beyond the respect people felt for their skills.

> **To avoid famine, reserve supplies of food were cached for use when food was scarce.**

FURTHER UNDERSTANDING

Tundra Treeless arctic plains that make up the area between the tree line and the icecap. The subsoil is permanently frozen, and there are almost no living plants, with the exception of mosses, lichens, and small flowering shrubs.

Pemmican To prepare this food, meat was dried in the open air or over a fire. It was then pounded into a powder and mixed with melted fat, and sometimes berries. This was an effective way to preserve meat, enabling it to last a long time. Once the mixture was cool, it was sewn into bison-hide bags. Pemmican could be stored or transported over long distances. Later, the English Navy used pemmican as their food source for Arctic expeditions.

■ The Kutcha-Kutchi was a ceremonial dance practised by the Kutchin. The Kutchin made their home in Canada's Western Subarctic.

7

Hunters of the Eastern SUBARCTIC

In summer, travel across the eastern woodlands would have been difficult without the birchbark canoe.

The Aboriginal groups of the Eastern Subarctic lived a hunting lifestyle. These groups were members of the Algonquian language base, and included the Beothuk, Naskapi, Montagnais, Algonquin, Ojibwa, and Cree. These peoples travelled over a large wooded area that stretched from present-day Alberta to the Atlantic Ocean, and from James Bay to the Great Lakes. This rugged country is covered with dense forests, lakes, and rivers. Except for a few places near the Atlantic Ocean, it is a land of rocks and **muskeg**, which is not suitable for farming. In summer, travel across the eastern woodlands would have been difficult without the birchbark canoe, an Algonquian invention.

In winter, Algonquians travelled across the deep snow on snowshoes, pulling their belongings on toboggans.

Since the Algonquians hunted and fished for their food, their wigwams and birchbark lodges had to be simply built for quick assembly and portability. What they hunted depended on what was available in their area. Moose meat was a favourite food. Traps or snares were used to catch bears, deers, beavers, and rabbits. Fishing was also important, and a variety of bone hooks, spears, nets, and wicker traps were used. Along the eastern coast, harpoons were used to kill seals and whales. Wild rice and berries were also a part of the diet, when they were available. Maple sugar was enjoyed by certain groups, such as the Ojibwa.

FURTHER UNDERSTANDING

Maple sugar Maple sap was tapped, or harvested, from maple trees in spring. A hole was created in the trunk of a sugar maple tree. The sap came out through a small spout and was collected in a container that hung from the tree. When the sap was heated, the water evaporated and left a syrup. Boiling the sap makes maple sugar.

Wigwams These portable homes were built by tying poles together with bark to create a dome-shaped frame. The frame was covered with animal hides, bark, or mats made of reeds. There were different sizes and shapes of wigwams, which depended on the size of the family. Wigwams were often decorated with colourful designs. The teepee, used by the Plains peoples, was also made with poles, but these were joined at the top and spread out at ground level to form a cone shape. The frame was then covered with animal hides.

■ The land occupied by the Cree is larger than any other Aboriginal group. It stretches from present-day Alberta to Québec.

The Algonquians lived in small family hunting groups during winter months. Each group needed a large area in which they could find enough food. Large groups living in one area could have exhausted the resources. To prevent this from occurring, small groups ensured balance. In summer, when food was plentiful, related families formed larger bands. Bands regularly gathered for feasts, games, songs, and dances.

Moccasins, leggings, shirts, and **breechcloths** were made of animal skins. Pieces of deerskin were carefully cut to fit. They were then sewn together using bone **awls**, which made holes through which threads made of sinew were pushed. Clothes were often decorated with quills.

In cold weather, the Algonquians wore fur robes. These were also used as blankets or beds for sleeping. Babies slept wrapped in moss bags or tucked in cradle-boards that could be hung from a low bough or carried on the mother's back.

Decisions were made after discussions at special meetings held by elders. Leaders were usually men who were respected for their wisdom and experience. They had little direct authority, but ruled by setting a good example. Laws were based on customs and traditions. When an injustice occurred, it was customary for the guilty person to offer gifts to the person who had been wronged.

RESPECT FOR GAME

Most Algonquians treated game animals with respect. Bears were much esteemed for their great strength, the danger they posed to humans, their human-like form when standing on their hind legs, and their intelligence. The remains of game animals, such as beaks, bones, claws, and skulls, were kept in a safe place. Since these remains were thought to bring good fortune to the bearer, they were sometimes carried in special bags.

■ The Ojibwa gathered wild rice that grew in streams, lakes, and marshes. They harvested the rice by knocking it off the plants into their canoes.

Fishers of the Northwest COAST

Totem poles, masks, and sculptures showcased the talented carving skills of the Pacific Coast Aboriginal groups.

Seven major groups belonging to five different language bases lived along the Northwest Coast of the Pacific Ocean. These groups included the Coast Salish, the Bella Coola, the Kwakiutl, the Nootka, the Tsimshian, the Tlingit, and the Haida.

The Northwest Coast has a wet climate. Heavy rainfalls have produced dense forests and many rivers and streams. This garden of Canada provided a year-round food supply for the groups living in the area. The majority of the food came from sea animals. Land animals were also eaten, as well as vegetables that were taken from land and sea. Many foods were dried for use in winter. Preserved foods were distributed at winter feasts.

The Pacific Coast peoples lived in large houses that were constructed out of red cedar planks. The plank houses were usually arranged in rows along the sea, with their entrances facing the water. The central doorway consisted of an opening at the bottom of a carved totem pole. Several related families, called clans, shared one plank house.

Water travel by canoe was the primary means of transportation. Canoes varied in size and style, according to how they were used. For short hunting trips, small dugouts were the most practical. For long ocean voyages and for wars, red cedar logs provided large canoe materials. Some Haida war canoes measured as long as 18 to 21 metres.

It was in art that these groups excelled. Totem poles, masks, and sculptures showcased their carving skills. These great carpenters also built boxes, chests, and bowls out of wood. Many objects were beautifully decorated and skillfully painted. Blankets made of goat wool and dog fur were covered in finely woven designs and patterns.

■ Some totem poles in British Columbia are more than 250 years old and measure up to 20 metres tall.

FURTHER UNDERSTANDING

Plank houses The peoples of the Northwest Coast took advantage of the area's vast supply of trees to build massive houses with planks taken from red cedars. These groups typically lived in permanent homes in winter, moving into portable homes closer to food sources in summer. Most of the houses in a village were owned by the elite—nobles and chiefs. The houses were considered expressions of the owner's status and were ornately decorated.

Totem poles Large tree trunks carved out of cedar were used to show a group's rank, or standing, in the community. Peoples of the Northwest Coast carved symbols, such as animals, fish, and birds, to represent their family history.

The Pacific Potlatch

Since food was so plentiful and so readily available, the Northwest Coast groups had plenty of spare time. As this was especially true during winter, there was much feasting and dancing.

For the peoples of the Northwest Coast, the potlatch ceremony was a vital part of their culture. It was a gift-giving **ritual**. Chiefs and nobles gave potlatches to announce important events, such as marriages, rights to fishing and hunting territories, or the creation of new songs, dances, or dramas. Everybody in the clan was involved in planning and carrying out a potlatch. Hosts often spent years making and collecting items to be given away as gifts. Each guest was given a gift such as a woven blanket, a fur, a robe, a carving, a canoe, or a copper shield. This practice confirmed the host's status as a person rich enough to give away possessions.

On the day of the event, the hosts dressed in their finest clothes. The guests were formally greeted by the hosts, and were seated according to their rank.

Dances, songs, and speeches praising the visitors were followed by feasting that might last as long as two weeks. As many as 500 guests might be invited. Later, guests invited their host to a potlatch given in the first host's honour. This ritual of generosity ensured that everyone shared in the riches of their region.

■ Artist Joanna S. Wilson is one of the few painters to have captured potlatch ceremonies on canvas.

Fishers and Hunters of the Interior
PLATEAU

> Salmon were treated with great respect—the Interior Salish even had a special ceremony to welcome the first salmon of the season.

Nestled in a giant cradle of mountainous land between the Coastal Range and the Rocky Mountains, lived eight Aboriginal groups belonging to four different language bases. These groups tended to borrow cultural customs from neighbouring areas. The Kootenays, who had once lived on the Prairies, were eventually pushed out by the Siksika, and settled in southeastern British Columbia. They spoke their own language, but kept many of the customs and traditions of the Plains groups. In their new location, the Kootenays learned from the Interior Salish to weave baskets and build canoes.

The Interior Salish spoke dialects of the Salishan language base. Included in this group were the Lilloet, Thompson, Okanagan, Lake, and Shuswap. The Lilloet were great traders, exchanging goods between the coastal and the interior Aboriginal groups. From the Interior Salish and the Kootenays, they obtained mountain goat wool, dried berries, skins, and jade for trade. From the coastal groups, they obtained ornaments, wooden boxes, and pestles for grinding berries.

Fish—especially salmon—were an important food for the interior groups. Special two-pronged fishing spears were used by some groups, while others used a fishing **gaff**. Spawning salmon were caught in dip nets and weirs. Salmon were treated with great respect—the Interior Salish even had a special ceremony to welcome the first salmon of the season. Game animals, roots, and berries were other food sources. Moose were hunted in the north, and elk were hunted in the south. Bears, caribou, and deer were found on the lower slopes. Mountain goats and mountain sheep lived high in the mountains. These groups also ate smaller animals such as beavers, ducks, geese, groundhogs, grouse, porcupines, and rabbits. Preserving foods for winter months was very important for survival. The Interior groups dried roots

FURTHER UNDERSTANDING

Weirs Large traps or fences, made of tree branches or wooden poles, were placed across a stream to catch fish. Once the fish were trapped, they could be easily speared.

■ A salmon weir could catch up to 1,000 fish per day. Similar weirs could be made to catch other types of fish, muskrat, or beaver.

and berries, and smoked or dried meats and fish. Caches of frozen or dried meat were hidden high in the trees, and fish and berries were stored in deep pits.

Clothing was made of deerskin or moosehide, and fur robes were worn in the winter. The Interior Salish made some clothes of bark and of mountain goat wool. Necklaces and bracelets were very popular, and faces were painted with designs revealed in dreams and visions. Some groups practised tattooing.

Government was informal. Groups were divided into smaller bands. Each band had its own council. Elders, who knew the best berry grounds, fishing places, and hunting territories, had the most influence.

Homes and Transportation

The Interior groups built a variety of homes. The Interior Salish lived in warm, underground winter homes, and moved into cone-shaped tents in summer. Northern groups built log or pole huts, much like those of the coastal groups. The Kootenays preferred to live in Plains-like teepees. The Athapaskan groups, who lived to the north and south of this area, built double **lean-tos**, often with a fire burning between them. Furniture consisted of mats woven from reeds, and some groups used animal skins for sleeping.

The rugged landscape made transportation difficult. Even with a variety of birchbark canoes, cedar dugouts, and animal-skin boats, water travel through rapids and narrow passages was difficult. On land, dogs helped carry cargo and pull toboggans. Snowshoes were used by some groups. After horses were introduced in the 1800s, they became very popular with groups in the southern region.

■ In summer, the Kootenays would cover their teepees with light mats woven from reeds.

Bison Hunters of the PLAINS

Life on the Prairies changed dramatically with the arrival of horses.

The Plains east of the Rocky Mountains were the home of several Aboriginal groups, whose lifestyles were based on the great herds of bison. These groups shared a similar culture, but did not speak the same language. The Blackfoot Nation was an alliance of three smaller groups—the Siksika, the Kainai, and the Pikuni. Together, they formed the largest and strongest of the prairie groups.

Before they were introduced to horses, the Plains peoples walked everywhere, carrying their belongings on their backs or using dogs to pull a travois. Life on the Prairies changed dramatically with the arrival of horses. Travelling became much easier and faster. Since horses could pull or carry heavy loads, the Plains groups could build bigger teepees. They could keep larger supplies of food and clothing. Horses became an important sign of wealth.

Plains groups were made up of smaller units, called bands, that were headed by chiefs. Most bands were composed of family units that hunted and travelled together. When bands gathered to attend a meeting, they pitched their teepees in a circle, with the council teepee in the centre. The council was made up of chiefs from the various bands as well as elders.

Religion was an important part of the Plains cultural life. Each spring, the bands reunited at a gathering, which included special dances and ceremonies. One important spiritual ceremony, held in midsummer, was the Sun Dance. It was usually arranged by an individual as a request for spiritual help or in response to a vision.

FURTHER UNDERSTANDING

Sun Dance Among some Plains groups, women were responsible for arranging the Sun Dance. After four days of preparation and ritual, the Sun Dance lasted another four days. Most of Sun Dance was spent setting up a sacred dance pole and lodge. On the final day, people danced many special dances. Some dances involved self-torture, so Sun Dancers enjoyed great prestige and respect in their community. The Sun Dance was a time to renew bonds within the community.

Travois A travois consisted of two long poles, each tied to the sides of a dog or a horse. The poles dragged behind, and a framework near the back carried goods.

■ The Plains teepees were easily moved, yet were strong enough to resist the elements.

THE BISON HUNT

Bison hunts were carefully organized affairs, requiring the co-operation of all band members. Various methods were used by different groups. Before the Plains groups had horses, men dressed in wolf skins steered a small herd of bison toward two lines of people who were lying on the ground in a V-shape formation. Suddenly, they stood up, and their shouts and waves stampeded the frightened herd into a circular compound or corral made of logs. Other groups preferred to drive a bison herd to the edge of a steep cliff, forcing them to fall to their deaths.

Bison jumps and corrals were replaced by the "surround method" after the Aboriginal peoples obtained rifles and horses. Hunters on horseback galloped in circles around a bison herd, firing at the animals as they passed.

Every part of the bison was used. Bison meat was roasted, boiled, smoked, dried, or made into pemmican. The tail could become a whip, an ornament, or a fly whisk. Tanned hides made robes or blankets. With the hair removed, tanned bison skins were used to make all kinds of clothing including, moccasins, leggings, breechcloths, shirts, belts, and caps. Sewn together, bison hides covered teepees. Warriors used the tougher hides to make shields. Bison horns became cups, bowls, and spoons. Their bladders became storage containers, and their stomachs became cooking pots. Cutting and scraping tools, as well as toys, were made of bison bones. Dried bison dung was used as fuel for fires.

■ Although they had to be careful to avoid being killed by falling bison, hunters waited at the base of the cliffs to kill and butcher the animals.

The Dawn of Canada

15

Farmers of the Northeastern
WOODLANDS

There was little danger of famine, so the farmers built permanent villages.

The Aboriginal peoples of the Northeastern Woodlands were divided into two main groups. One group, comprised of the Hurons, the Neutral, and the Tobacco Nation, lived in what is now Ontario. The second group, the Iroquois Confederacy, lived south of the Great Lakes and along the St. Lawrence River Valley. The Iroquois were organized into the League of Five Nations, which included the Cayuga, Mohawk, Oneida, Onondaga, and the Seneca. When the Tuscarora joined the confederacy in the early 1700s, it became known as the League of Six Nations. Together they formed one of the oldest **democratic** societies in the world. Both groups spoke dialects of the Iroquoian language.

The fertile soil around the Great Lakes was ideal for agriculture. During long summers, the Huron and the Iroquois grew corn, beans, squash, pumpkins, artichokes, tobacco, and sunflowers. There were large forests in which they could hunt. Trees were cut down to make room for fields where they could grow food. As well as farming and hunting, they fished in the Great Lakes. There was little danger of famine and no need to travel very far to find food, so these farmers built permanent villages.

The Iroquoian system of government was very well developed. Women played an important role. Women owned houses and land, and descent was traced through the female line. Although men were the leaders and decision makers, they were usually appointed by the head woman in the village. They could replace a chief, known as a **sachem**, if he did not do his job well. Both the Huron and the Neutral nations were unions of several groups, with elected councils. In each village, the council was made up of clan chiefs. In the formal council meetings, decisions were

FURTHER UNDERSTANDING

League of Five Nations
The league was governed by fifty chiefs, called sachems. They met every August or September to discuss important issues. The Iroquois used the idea of a longhouse to describe their league. The Onondaga, who lived in the centre of the Iroquois territory, were the "Keepers of the Fire" in the longhouse. The Seneca represented the western door of the longhouse, and the Mohawk represented the eastern door. At meetings, the sachems had special places in which to sit, according to their place in the longhouse. As a result of their special position, the Onondaga were in charge of keeping the historical records of the league. The Onondaga chief was the head of the League of the Iroquois.

Longhouses Longhouses were built around large poles, which were set in the ground. The poles were curved toward the centre and attached together to create a roof. Outside, walls were covered with bark. Inside, sections were created on both sides of a long corridor. Each family lived in their own section, but shared a fire with the family across the corridor. Food was hung from the roof.

■ In the Iroquoian farming nations, women were responsible for keeping birds away from crops.

democratically made after much eloquent discussion and debate. Peace and order in the villages were maintained through custom and tradition.

Daily Life

The Huron and Iroquois lived in villages, some of which were quite large. Several families lived together in bark-covered longhouses. Inside, there was room for several cooking fires and many sleeping platforms. Longhouses had room to store food, weapons, clothing, and tools. Dried foods were often hung from the ceiling or stored in pits that were dug into the earth floor. There were storage porches at each end of the longhouse.

Women planted and harvested crops. They also did the cooking, and gathered nuts and berries from the woods near their homes. They made clothing, and clay and wooden containers. They also raised the children. Men cleared the fields and built canoes, tools, and weapons. They also hunted, fished, and protected the villages from harm. The men travelled to trade their extra food for furs, hides, and other goods.

The Huron and the Iroquois made their clothing from deer hides and beaver pelts. Clothes were decorated with paint or porcupine quill designs. Bracelets, necklaces, and earrings were made from shell beads. While the women wore their hair in a single braid, the men had several different hairstyles. Some men shaved the sides of their head, leaving a strip of hair down the middle. Others shaved only one side of their head and left long hair on the other.

■ In the eighteenth century, longhouses were replaced by single-family dwellings. Longhouses continued to be used for political and ceremonial purposes.

CANADA'S First Peoples

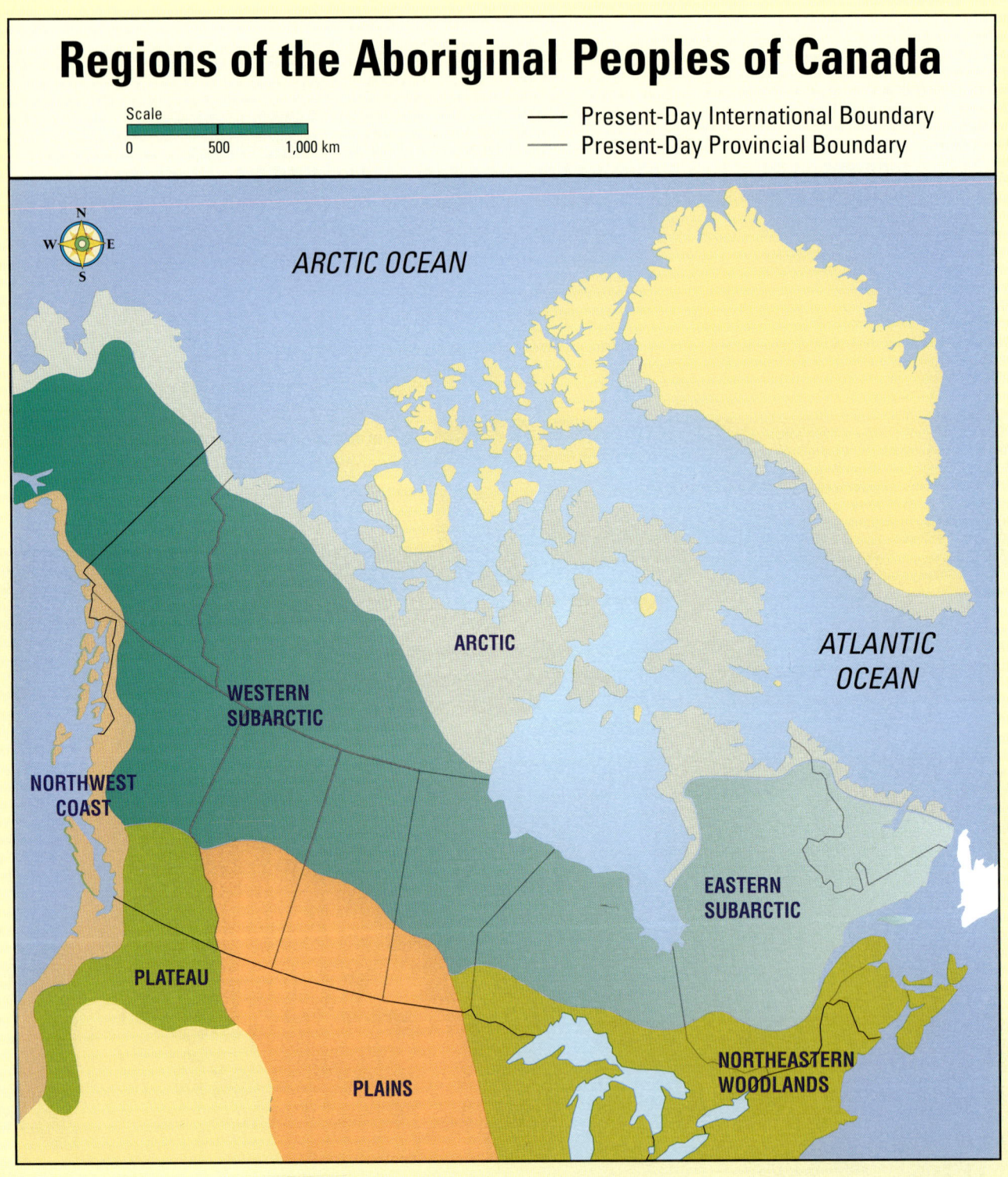

Aboriginal Peoples

ARCTIC
- **Groups:** Inuit peoples: Baffin Island, Caribou, Copper, Iglulik, Hudson Bay, Labrador, Mackenzie, Netsilik, Polar, Sadlermiut
- **Land and climate:** long winters, cold, no trees, some areas permanently frozen all year
- **Homes:** igloos, tents in summer
- **Transportation:** kayak, dog sleds
- **Food:** reliance on animal rather than plant foods; seals and other sea mammals
- **Other:** co-operation is key feature of culture

NORTHWEST COAST
- **Groups:** Bella Coola, Coast Salish, Haida, Kwakiutl, Nootka, Tlingit, Tsimshian
- **Land and climate:** mild, wet, heavily forested
- **Homes:** permanent cedar longhouses
- **Transportation:** dugout canoes
- **Food:** sea animals, some land animals, plants from land and sea
- **Other:** artwork, such as totem poles; potlatch ceremonies to share wealth

INTERIOR PLATEAU
- **Groups:** Carrier, Chilcotin, Interior Salish, Kootenay, Tagish, Tsetsaut
- **Land and climate:** varied, from forested to dry and desert-like, rivers and some lakes, surrounded by mountains
- **Homes:** various, depending on climate, from plains-like teepees to wooden longhouses
- **Transportation:** various canoes and boats, toboggans, snowshoes
- **Food:** mountain animals, salmon
- **Other:** groups adapted some ways of life of other groups

EASTERN SUBARCTIC
- **Groups:** Algonquin, Beothuk, Naskapi, Nehiyawak and Nihiyawak (Cree), Montagnais, Ojibwa, and Ottawa
- **Land and climate:** dense forest with lakes, rivers, rocks, muskeg
- **Homes:** portable wigwams, birchbark lodges
- **Transportation:** birchbark canoes, snowshoes for winter
- **Food:** forest animals, fish, rice, and maple sugar
- **Other:** travelled in small hunting groups to avoid exhausting resources

PLAINS
- **Groups:** Nakoda (Stony), Blackfoot Nation: Siksika (Blackfoot), Kainai (Blood), Pikuni (Peigan), Gros Ventre
- **Land and climate:** harsh winters, warm summers, open regions with some rivers, few lakes
- **Homes:** portable teepees
- **Transportation:** foot and dog, travois, and later reliance on horse
- **Food:** bison
- **Other:** various bison hunt techniques, Sun Dance

NORTHEASTERN WOODLANDS
- **Groups:** Erie, Huron, Iroquois Confederacy, Mi'kmaq, Neutral, Petun, Stadaconans, Tobacco Nation
- **Land and climate:** fertile soil for agriculture, many forests and lakes
- **Homes:** permanent longhouses
- **Transportation:** snowshoes in winter, canoes in summer
- **Food:** fish, agricultural products, meat from hunting and trapping
- **Other:** highly organized democratic government, traded with other Aboriginal groups

WESTERN SUBARCTIC
- **Groups:** Dene (Chipewyan), Dogrib, Dunne-za (Beaver), Hare, Kutchin, Sekani, Slavey, Tahltan, Yellowknife
- **Land and climate:** forests, tundra, some ground permanently frozen
- **Homes:** portable lean-tos
- **Transportation:** snowshoes, toboggans, canoe, or foot
- **Food:** reliance on caribou
- **Other:** lived mainly on edge of forest, moved into forest in winter, onto treeless tundra plains to hunt caribou in summer

Arrival of the VIKINGS

The Vikings sailed the coasts of Europe in their sleek long ships, which were decorated with a carved dragon head on the prow.

Aboriginal peoples adapted their lifestyles to their environments. They were effectively meeting their economic, social, and political needs in diverse ways. They had the potential to be a great source of knowledge and assistance to Europeans explorers, who were unfamiliar with North America's environment. Contact between Aboriginal peoples and the Europeans involved co-operation and conflict, and led to many changes for both cultures.

The Vikings Reach Vinland

About one thousand years ago, most Europeans lived in fear of Viking raids. The Vikings, or Norsemen, were the ancestors of present-day Scandinavians who live in Denmark, Norway, and Sweden. At the beginning of the ninth century, the Norse homelands became overcrowded. The more daring of the Vikings took to the seas in search of new farmlands, adventure, and profit. They sailed the coasts of Europe in their sleek long ships, or drakkars, which were decorated with striped sails and a carved dragon head on the prow. The Vikings plundered and looted the seaport towns on the coast along the Atlantic Ocean and the North Sea. Sometimes, they built settlements in the rich countries they had conquered.

Two Viking **sagas** tell about Vinland, the first Viking settlement in North America: *The Saga of Erik the Red* and *The Saga of the Greenlanders*. These two accounts are not strictly accurate. Like many stories told orally over the years, the accounts were likely changed and embellished. Historians use the accounts like pieces of a jigsaw puzzle to speculate about the actual events.

FURTHER UNDERSTANDING

Erik the Red *The Saga of Erik the Red* tells the tale of Erik Thorvaldsson, known as Erik the Red. Erik was a convicted murderer who fled from Norway to Iceland. In 982 AD, Erik was banished from Iceland for three years. Forced to find a new home, Erik sailed west and eventually came to an unknown land, which he called Greenland. He hoped such an attractive name would convince others to join him in starting a new colony. He was successful and, in 986 AD, Erik and his followers established two settlements in Greenland. These colonies thrived until the fifteenth century.

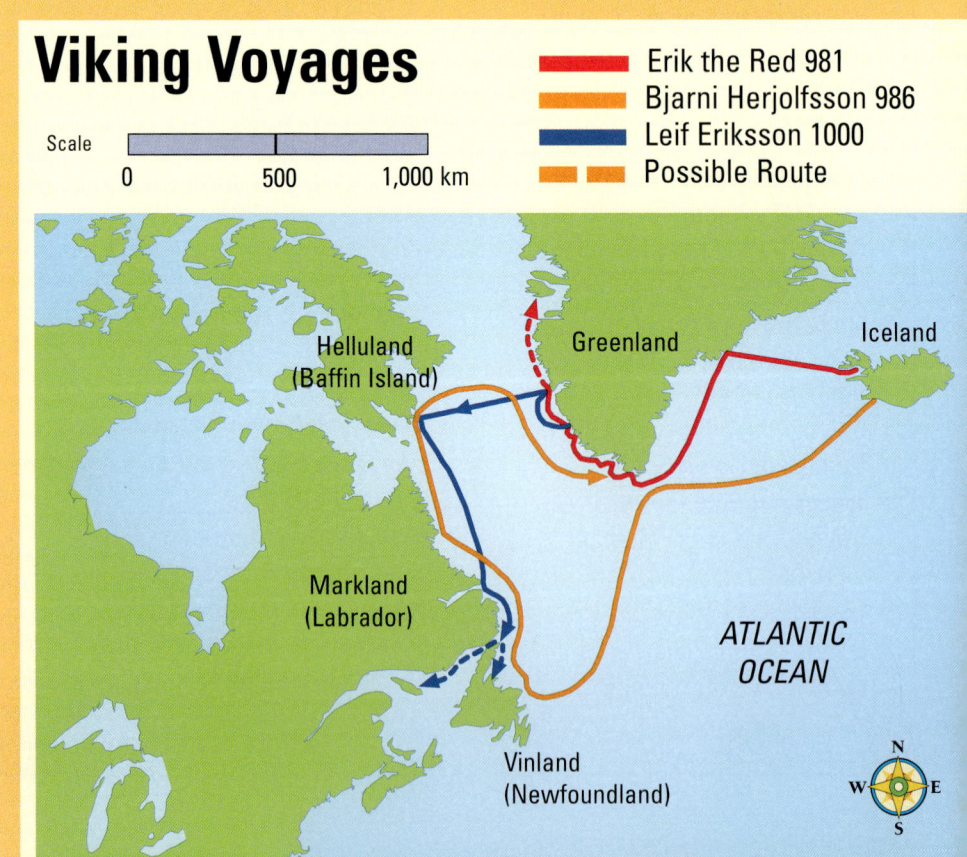

The Saga of the Greenlanders

The *Saga of the Greenlanders* describes how a young Icelander, named Bjarni Herjulfsson, came to be the first European to see the North American coastline. Bjarni was a prosperous trader. After one trading voyage, he returned to Norway to learn that his father had left for Greenland with Erik the Red. Although they had never been there before, Bjarni and his crew decided to follow.

Soon after they set out on the journey, violent storms drove their ship far off course. Then, they were lost in a heavy fog. After several days at sea, they finally saw land. They could see low hills covered with forests, but Bjarni would not allow his crew to go ashore. They continued sailing northward, passing by the coast of a land that appeared flat and thickly wooded. Again, Bjarni refused to let his crew go ashore.

They spent more days at sea, fighting gales and rough waters. Eventually, they came to a new land of mountains and glaciers that Bjarni guessed was Greenland. At last, he and his crew went ashore, where they found Bjarni's father's ship and the Norse settlement.

While Bjarni did not wish to explore the new lands he had sighted, other Greenlanders became curious when they heard the account of his journey. Around 1001, Leif Eriksson, the son of Erik the Red, set out to explore the lands Bjarni had seen. It is believed that they travelled from what is now Baffin Island, to Labrador, and then to northern Newfoundland.

Leif and his crew decided to spend the winter at this new site. One day a German member of the crew named Tyrkir disappeared. Just as the crew was beginning to worry, an excited Tyrkir returned to camp. He carried some vines and fruits that he thought were grapes, for he had seen many varieties of grapes growing in Germany. Leif decided to call this new land "Vinland." When spring came, they loaded their ships with timber that they had cut, for timber was scarce in Greenland. Then, they sailed back to Greenland.

■ Leif Eriksson was one of the first Vikings to land in North America. Bjarni Herjulfsson's reports of a heavily wooded coastline were an irresistible lure to the timber-needy Norse.

The Vikings Meet the SKRAELINGS

> *Without warning, the Vikings attacked, killing all but one who managed to escape.*

In 1004, Thorvald Eriksson, Leif's brother, headed the second expedition to Vinland. He was likely the first European to meet Aboriginal people, who the Vikings called *Skraelings*. This name meant "barbarians."

Thorvald's group came across nine people who were asleep under three animal-skin boats. Without warning, the Vikings attacked them, killing all but one who managed to escape. Before long, he returned to the Viking camp with his own people and a fleet of war canoes. During the battle that followed, Thorvald was killed by a Beothuk arrow. After his burial, his crew returned to Greenland.

In 1011, Gudrid and her husband, Thorfun Karlsefni, sailed for Vinland with three ships. The party included livestock and a group of settlers, including several women. A severe winter followed, and in spring, Karlsefni and his group moved south to a bay that they called Hop, where they became friendly with the local Aboriginal people.

Later, in a misunderstanding over some missing weapons, the Viking settlers killed one of the Aboriginal people. The man's relatives returned seeking revenge. They attacked the Vikings, who fled in panic. The Vikings spent their third and last winter at the settlement before returning to Greenland. Snorri, Karlsefni's son, was most likely the first European child born in North America.

The story of the Viking discovery and settlement of North America is full of mystery. No one else in Europe at the time seemed to know about the voyages. According to historians, when Christopher Columbus set out on his well-known voyage across the Atlantic Ocean in 1492, most Europeans had never heard of Vinland. Today, experts believe that Norse ruins found at L'Anse aux Meadows could mark the location of Vinland.

FURTHER UNDERSTANDING

L'Anse aux Meadows
The site at L'Anse aux Meadows was found on the north coast of Newfoundland in 1960 by a Norwegian explorer, Helge Ingstad. He and his wife, Anne Stine Ingstad, along with a national historic parks branch of the federal government, excavated the site. Artifacts included such items as a glass bead, a bronze pin, and an iron smithy. Remains of a sod house were also found. Evidence from the site indicates that forty to fifty people lived there for almost ten years.

■ Each one of Thorvald Eriksson's small ships could hold no more than thirty people. Even if the Greenlanders had a fleet of ten ships, they would still have been badly outnumbered.

An Age of DISCOVERY

While the Vikings roamed the northern seas of Europe and explored the northeast coasts of Canada, most Europeans were too busy fighting off invasions to think of discovering new lands. At this time, Europe was organized by a feudal system of land ownership. During the feudal years, people's lives were constantly threatened by famine, disease, and war. They knew little about the rest of the world.

A renewed interest in knowledge, the arts, and the cultures of the world was awakening in Europe. This awakening, or rebirth, is known as the Renaissance, and lasted from about 1450 to the early 1600s. It was a period of discovery. During the Renaissance, Europeans began to learn about other countries, and sought the fine silks, embroideries, cloths, and spices that came from places such as India and China. Western European merchants and traders sought a shorter and cheaper route to the Far East that avoided the difficult and dangerous land route across Europe and Asia. Larger, more seaworthy ships were constructed. Improved navigational devices, such as the compass, **sextant**, and **astrolabe**, made sailing easier. Yet, even after the discovery of the southern sea route around Africa, ocean travel to the Far East remained a long, dangerous, and costly journey.

> Most Europeans were too busy fighting off invasions to think of discovering new lands.

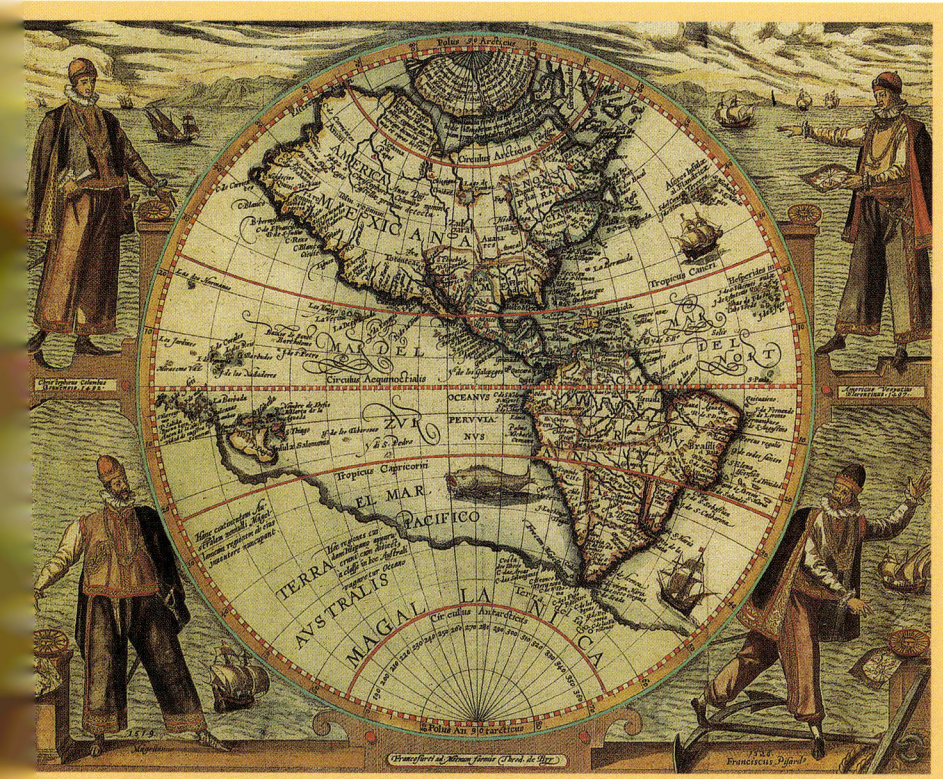

■ Theodore de Bry's New World Map of 1596 shows the world as it was perceived during the Age of Discovery.

FURTHER UNDERSTANDING

Feudal system Nearly all of western Europe was organized into small, local estates. At the top of the social order was the king. To defend his domain, the king divided his land into smaller holdings that were ruled by dukes, counts, and lords. In return for the use of the land, these noblemen pledged their allegiance to the king. In times of war, which were frequent, the nobles supplied the king with an army. The serfs, or peasants, who lived on the land had individual agreements with the nobleman. Serfs were expected to work the land for the nobleman and to submit all payments and taxes that he demanded. In exchange for their taxes and labour, the serfs received shelter and a promise of protection from the nobleman.

23

Columbus Sets SAIL

Columbus helped Spain become the richest nation in Europe.

During the Renaissance, navigators and scientists began to claim that the world was round. Until then, people believed that the world was flat and that if a ship sailed too far out to sea, it would fall off the edge. Among the navigators who believed that the world was round were some who insisted that the Atlantic Ocean was only a small body of water, and that the distance between Spain and India could be covered by a sailing vessel in a few days.

A new map that charted such theories, called the Behaim Globe, appeared in Nuremberg, Germany in 1492. It depicted only a few scattered islands between Europe and Asia. Navigators and traders reasoned that, if indeed the world was round, a different and shorter route to the Far East could be found across this "small" ocean.

Portugal and Spain, two of the strongest seafaring nations, led the search to find an ocean passage to the Far East. Christopher Columbus, an Italian navigator, was commissioned by the queen of Spain to find a shorter route westward across the Atlantic Ocean. In 1492, Columbus and his crew set off with three small vessels.

Columbus estimated that the voyage would take about one week. Instead, it took seventy-one days. Finally, he landed on an island in the Caribbean. Columbus thought he had found the East Indies. In later voyages, Columbus sailed along the coasts of Central and South America. Until his death in 1506, he believed that he had reached Asia. Although he was mistaken, his explorations of the Americas helped Spain become the richest nation in Europe.

Portuguese sailors followed the Spanish ships across the Atlantic Ocean and soon also traded in the Americas. It was not long before the two rivals had to sign a treaty that divided their discoveries in what the Europeans referred to as the "New World."

FURTHER UNDERSTANDING

Spain During the Age of Discovery, European kings and queens were willing to invest money in exploration. Through it, they hoped they would gain power and riches. In 1492, Christopher Columbus set out on a voyage to Asia. His trips westward eventually landed him in South America. Subsequently, Spain made many voyages to the Americas. A treaty between Spain and Portugal, signed in 1494, gave the Spanish control over large parts of North and South America. Their power and wealth grew as they discovered gold, silver, and other riches in this "New World."

East Indies The term *Indies* was first used in the 1400s. At the time it referred to southeastern Asia—including India, Burma, Thailand, Laos, Cambodia, and Vietnam—as well as the Philippines, and the Malay Archipelago. Columbus believed he had landed in the Indies when he discovered America. As a result, he named the islands he discovered the "Caribbean Indies." Today, the Caribbean Indies are known as the West Indies, while the East Indies primarily refer to the islands of the Malay Archipelago.

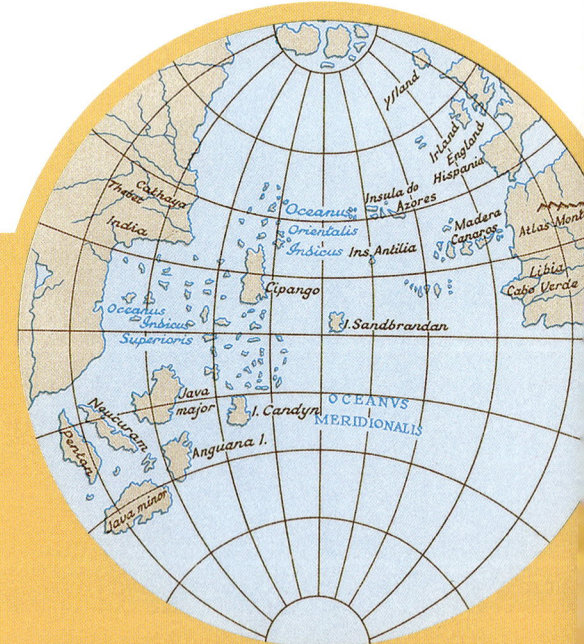

■ The Behaim Globe of 1492 is similar to the one Columbus used during his voyage west in the same year. There is no evidence that Columbus and Behaim ever met.

Life Aboard the Discovery Ships

Living conditions aboard the ships of discovery were appalling, not only by modern standards, but by the standards of the time. The ships leaked, and rats and roaches thrived. Poor sanitary habits meant that no area on a boat was clean. The stench was often overwhelming and filled all the living spaces. People slept where they could find room—with the exception of the captain, no one had sleeping quarters of their own.

Food was another problem. It was difficult to store enough food to feed the crews for such long ocean voyages. People ate dried or salted meat and fish, biscuits, rice, dried peas, cheese, and onions. Garlic, oil, vinegar, water, and wine were added to the menu. The diet lacked in fruits and vegetables, and was high in salt. Even staples, such as grains or flour, swarmed with insects or were covered with mould long before the end of the voyage.

Water casks often sprung leaks, depleting the critical supply of fresh water.

Sailors used the Sun and the stars to navigate. On cloudy nights or foggy days, a ship could easily become lost. Vessels were often wrecked or blown hundreds of kilometres off course in a storm. The only source of power was wind and sail.

Christopher Columbus's First Voyage

■ Columbus opened the Americas to European exploration.

Cabot Rediscovers CANADA

> The crew scooped a big basket full of fresh Atlantic cod out of the ocean and had a feast.

News of Columbus's voyages spread across Europe. Another Italian sea captain, Giovanni Caboto, was sailing English ships. In England he was known as John Cabot. Cabot shared Columbus's dream of finding a route to Asia by sailing west across the Atlantic Ocean. Merchants from Bristol, England, were willing to provide him with a ship and a crew with which to make the attempt. King Henry VII of England gave him permission to explore and claim for England all new lands he might discover. In May 1497, Cabot and his crew of eighteen sailed from Bristol on the ship *Matthew*. After fifty-four days at sea, they sighted land. Like the Vikings before him, Cabot had discovered Newfoundland. He claimed the land for England. He became the first person to begin England's claims to land in North America.

As the *Matthew* sailed on, the ocean became shallow. The ship was surrounded by fish. The crew scooped a big basket full of fresh Atlantic cod out of the ocean and had a feast. Cabot had found a wonderful fishing area that later became known as the Grand Banks. The Grand Banks is an area of shallow water southeast of Newfoundland that stretches out for 500 kilometres. The water is between 40 and 200 metres deep.

Cabot returned to England and reported that he had reached India and had seen "Red Indians." Although he had returned with neither spices nor silk, the merchants were pleased about reports of codfish. They needed more food to sell, and cod was popular.

The king gave Cabot money for another trip. In 1498, Cabot set sail with five ships and more than 200 settlers. They never reached their destination. No one knows what happened to Cabot and the settlers. They were probably lost at sea.

FURTHER UNDERSTANDING

Red Indians The people Cabot saw were neither red nor Indian. They were likely Beothuks, Aboriginal people who lived in Newfoundland. The Beothuk protected themselves against insects by smearing their bodies and belongings with red clay. This practice was also a custom associated with their religious beliefs.

■ The actual spot of John Cabot's 1497 landing is unknown. It is likely that he and his crew landed in Labrador, Newfoundland, or Cape Breton.

EARLY FISHING TRADE

Although Cabot's voyage did not accomplish its original task, the Europeans now knew about the Grand Banks. Sailors began to fish there every summer, sailing back to Europe with a hold full of fish.

Fish was an important part of the Roman Catholic European diet. Religious teachings forbade Roman Catholics to eat meat on Fridays in memory of Christ's death on Good Friday. There were also about 150 other days each year when Roman Catholics were not permitted to eat meat. Since fish was not considered meat, it was in great demand. Cod was popular because it had little fat and did not rot as quickly as other fish.

Since the voyage was so long, fishers had to preserve their catches before they headed home. French crews heavily salted the cod and stored it on their ships. They rarely went ashore, except for fresh water and firewood. The English did not have as much salt as the French, so they used a different method of preservation. They cleaned and lightly salted the cod. Then, they dried the fish in the sun on racks they built on the shore. The dried cod was packed in barrels that could be shipped for sale anywhere—even to warm countries. The dried cod rarely spoiled.

Eventually, some English captains began to leave a few crew members on shore each winter to look after their fishing equipment. Several individuals stayed in Newfoundland for several winters. They built houses, and Newfoundland became their home.

■ In 1497, John Cabot reported the presence of codfish off Canada's East Coast in such numbers that they could be caught in buckets.

The Portuguese Explore
NORTH AMERICA

Corte-Real reached a coast where several rivers flowed out to the sea and pine trees grew as tall as ships' masts.

In Portugal, news of Cabot's exploration aroused fears that England would meddle in the lands that had already been claimed by Portugal. King Manuel of Portugal first sent João Fernandes to explore the area where Cabot had been.

In 1500, King Manuel ordered another adventurer, Gaspar Corte-Real, to visit the region. Corte-Real's expedition sailed north but was forced to return to Portugal when it came upon an ice pack off the coast of Greenland. In 1501, Corte-Real set sail again with three ships. He reached a coast where several rivers flowed out to the sea and pine trees grew as tall as ships' masts. Corte-Real and his crew captured about sixty Aboriginal men and women and brought them back to Portugal. The new arrivals created a sensation, as people gathered to marvel at the appearance and gentle manners of the Aboriginal people.

On his next voyage, Corte-Real's ship disappeared. By this time, Vasco da Gama had returned from his voyage around Africa to the spice lands of India. Once Portugal had gained control of the spice trade, it lost interest in North America. Although Portuguese fishers continued to fish off the Grand Banks, most major expeditions from Portugal headed south to find gold and silver, rather than north to find fish and fur.

Around 1520, a Portuguese sailor, named João Alvares Fagundes, believed that cod fishing was profitable enough to begin a colony in Newfoundland. He explored the southern coast of Newfoundland and possibly Nova Scotia. The following year Fagundes brought several families to the area and started a colony on the east coast of Cape Breton Island. No evidence of the settlement has ever been found.

FURTHER UNDERSTANDING

Portugal Although the Portuguese did not establish a permanent settlement in what was to become Canada, places such as Cape Race, Cape Spear, Cape Bonavista, and Cape Foggo bear names that date back to the Portuguese explorers. Fernandes was an Azorean landowner, or *labrador*. He is likely responsible for naming the northeastern coast of Canada "Labrador."

■ Angra do Heroísmo, on Terceira Island, was founded in the fifteenth century and was one of the main port cities in Portugal during the Age of Discovery.

The Dawn of Canada

Giovanni da VERRAZZANO

Until the mid-1500s, the French were interested only in the Atlantic fisheries. During the early 1500s, French ships joined other European fishing vessels in the annual harvest of cod from the Grand Banks. These fishers were among the first Europeans to come into contact with the Aboriginal peoples of the region.

In Europe, the French king, Francis I, heard reports that Spain was becoming wealthy from the trade of spices and goods brought from Asia. He decided that France should enter into trade with the Far East.

He hired an Italian navigator, Giovanni da Verrazzano, to lead the French expedition.

Verrazzano was certain that he would find a middle passage to the Far East, somewhere between Florida and the newly discovered lands to the north. Wealthy European bankers supplied the funds for the expedition, and in 1523, Verrazzano left France with four ships. Heavy storms soon drove him back and forced him to revise his plans. He sailed a second time with only one ship, a crew of fifty, and provisions for an eight-month voyage.

In March 1524, Verrazzano landed on the coast of North America, near what is now Florida. During the following weeks, Verrazzano explored the entire coast as far north as Cape Breton Island, before giving up his search and returning to France. He claimed the entire eastern coast of North America for France.

Verrazzano explored the entire coast as far north as Cape Breton Island.

■ Historians believe that Giovanni da Verrazzano was killed by Aboriginal peoples in the Caribbean.

FURTHER UNDERSTANDING

Spice trade The spice trade was very important as it was a potential source of great wealth. Spices helped preserve and add flavour to food. The Italian cities of Genoa and Venice became powerful because they were spice trade centres. Western European merchants and traders were seeking a shorter and less expensive ocean route to the riches of the Orient.

Cartier's Voyages of EXPLORATION

Cartier raised a large cross on the shore of the Gaspé Peninsula, claiming the land for France.

Despite the failure of early explorers to find a quicker route to Asia, the Europeans did not quit. Some explorers tried to sail northwest, around the newly discovered land. Others tried to find a route through it.

Jacques Cartier was a master sailor from St. Malo, France, who had been on several fishing trips to the Grand Banks. The French king hired him to search for gold and jewels in the new lands across the Atlantic Ocean, and to find the Northwest Passage to Asia.

Cartier made three voyages. He left France for his first voyage on April 30, 1534. He had two ships and a crew of sixty-one. It took Cartier twenty days to reach Newfoundland. He sailed around the north end of the island, down the west side, and into the Gulf of St. Lawrence. Cartier and his crew spent the summer exploring the Gulf of St. Lawrence, looking for the Northwest Passage. In June, he landed on Prince Edward Island. He also explored several large bays along the coast of New Brunswick, in hopes that one of them might lead to the passage.

In July, Cartier landed on the Gaspé Peninsula and raised a large cross on the shore, claiming the land for France. There, he met a group of Iroquois, who had come to fish along the coast.

Their chief was named Donnacona. With him were his two sons, Taignoagny and Domagaya. Cartier gave Donnacona gifts of knives, glass beads, combs, and tin rings. In return, the Iroquois shared their food with the Europeans. They gave the visitors fresh fish. They also showed the Europeans how to cook the dried corn, fruits, and nuts they had brought with

FURTHER UNDERSTANDING

Aboriginal trade Before the Europeans came, many Aboriginal peoples met in summer to trade. They gathered where the Saguenay and St. Lawrence Rivers meet. European fishing crews were soon meeting there too. They began to trade knives, axes, and pots for the furs that the Aboriginals brought to trade.

In 1543, as Jacques Cartier sailed past New Brunswick, he met the Mi'kmaq, who were eager to trade with the French. French traders were soon regularly sailing up the St. Lawrence River, in search of more trading opportunities.

Northwest Passage Early explorers had hoped that they would find a faster water route to Asia by sailing west across the Atlantic Ocean. England and France sent explorers to find a route across, or around, North America. Even though the desired route would not be found until 1845, many areas, such as the St. Lawrence River, Baffin Bay, Davis Strait, and Frobisher Bay, were explored as a result of their efforts.

■ Cartier's explorations of the St. Lawrence River first appeared on a world map in 1546.

30

them from their village, Stadacona—the site of present-day Québec City.

When Cartier returned to France for the winter, he captured Donnacona's sons to take back to France. He arrived in St. Malo, France, on September 4, 1534. After a winter in France, Cartier sailed back to North America in 1535. This time, he had three ships and a crew of 110 people. Domagaya and Taignoagny showed Cartier the route up the St. Lawrence River to their home. They arrived in Stadacona in September 1535.

Cartier explored farther up the river, past Stadacona. He found a second group of people living at Hochelaga, on the island of present-day Montréal. Cartier climbed a hill on the island and named it Mount Royal. From there he could see that the river stretched out a long way, but rapids would make travel by boat difficult. Cartier returned to Stadacona, where he and his crew spent the winter. Winter was much colder than the French were accustomed. Many of the French became sick, and twenty-five died. When Cartier sailed home in the spring, he took Donnacona, his two sons, and several other people with him.

Cartier's Final Voyage

In 1541, Cartier made his third and last voyage. He left France in May with five ships and 1,500 people. He wanted to start a settlement on the St. Lawrence River. Cartier and the settlers reached Stadacona in August.

The people of Stadacona were not happy to see Cartier return. He had used land near their homes without permission. He had visited Hochelaga against their wishes. He had not brought Donnacona and the others back from France.

Cartier spent another winter at a camp on the St. Lawrence River. The winter was hard for the settlers, and many died. He sailed home in June 1542. Cartier's goal to start a settlement had failed. More than sixty years passed before French explorers returned to the area.

■ Despite the help of the Iroquois, many of Cartier's men did not survive the harsh Canadian winter.

ABORIGINAL PEOPLES IN FRANCE

Trapped in France, Donnacona knew that the only way he would ever see his homeland again was if Cartier returned to North America. When Donnacona noticed that the king liked gold, diamonds, rubies, and other jewels, he boasted that he had seen many of them just north of his village. He also told stories of groups of people who flew through the trees like bats.

Donnacona was a good storyteller. It was partly due to his stories that the king sent Cartier back to North America in 1541. However, by this time, Donnacona and the other kidnapped Iroquois had died of European diseases.

The Search for the Northwest PASSAGE

When the Inuit defended themselves, one of their arrows wounded Frobisher.

English explorer Martin Frobisher was convinced that he could reach Asia by sailing northwest around North America. Queen Elizabeth I of England ordered a group of merchants to supply his ships for the journey.

Frobisher made his first trip in the summer of 1576. He explored the coast of Labrador. Then, he sailed farther north and discovered a bay near a large island. At first, Frobisher thought it may be the Northwest Passage. He named it Frobisher Bay.

One member of Frobisher's crew went ashore with gifts for the Inuit, who lived along the coast. The Inuit visited Frobisher's ship to trade their sealskin and bearskin coats for bells, mirrors, and other small articles. Using sign language, Frobisher asked one of them to guide his ship through the passage. The Inuk agreed. Five sailors went with him to retrieve his kayak so that he could guide them. Frobisher never saw his men again.

Before Frobisher returned to England, he kidnapped an Inuk man and his kayak. He also took back some rocks he had found along the shore. He thought they contained gold. Frobisher was eager to return to the area to search for gold. Merchants agreed to pay for another voyage.

On his second voyage in 1577, Frobisher and his crew collected 200 tonnes of the rock. Frobisher also tried to discover what had happened to the five sailors who had disappeared.

While some of Frobisher's crew were searching for gold, they met a group of Inuit and exchanged gifts with them. One day, when Frobisher and his crew started to leave, the Inuit followed. Thinking that they might know something about his missing crew, Frobisher tried to capture two of them. When the Inuit defended themselves, one of their arrows wounded Frobisher. The fight ended when Frobisher's crew captured one of the Inuit men.

FURTHER UNDERSTANDING

Iron Pyrite Since people often mistake iron pyrite for gold, it is sometimes called "fool's gold." Iron pyrite produces a foul odour when heated. This is one way to distinguish it from gold. Iron pyrite can be used to start a fire because it sparks when struck with an object, such as a hammer.

Inuk The word *Inuit* is from the Inuit-Inupiaq language and means "the people" or "real people." The word *Inuk* is the singular form of this word and refers to one member of the Inuit group.

■ Frobisher was one of Queen Elizabeth I's favourite privateers. As a privateer, Frobisher was given license to plunder the ships of England's enemies.

The Search Continues

Frobisher did not give up looking for his missing crew. One day he found an empty tent and thought it might have belonged to his men. His crew tried to catch a group of Inuit to ask about the tent. When the Inuit escaped in their kayaks, the English rowed after them, firing their guns. The Inuit landed and defended themselves from shore.

A fierce battle took place. The Inuit fought bravely, but their arrows were no match for the English guns. A few of the Inuit were killed. The English also captured two women and a baby. The English let one woman go, but took the mother and baby back to England. They also took the Inuk man they had captured earlier. All three became ill and died in England.

In 1578, Frobisher made his third voyage. This time he had fifteen ships. The ships were blown off course by storms and landed on an island. Again, Frobisher hauled tonnes of rocks back to England. There he received some bad news. The rocks were worthless. They contained no gold at all. It was iron pyrite.

Frobisher was discouraged and decided to stop exploring. He never learned what happened to the five missing sailors. Three hundred years later, an explorer from the United States heard an Inuit story about five Europeans who had come with the first ships. These men lived with the Inuit for a few years. Then, they built a large boat and sailed out into the open seas. They were never seen again.

■ On Frobisher's second voyage, he took an artist named John White along. White painted scenes of the troubled meetings between the English and the Inuit.

Champlain in NEW FRANCE

> **On several islands, the birds were so numerous that it was impossible to walk without stepping on their eggs.**

Samuel de Champlain was born in a fishing-port city in France in 1570. His father was a sea captain and much of Champlain's early life was spent sailing the north Atlantic Ocean. Although he had little formal education, Champlain became a skilled ship navigator and **cartographer**. In 1603, Champlain sailed to North America. His records of the trip were the first detailed accounts of the St. Lawrence since Cartier's voyages, sixty years earlier.

Champlain described the thick clouds of birds he saw in the Gulf of St. Lawrence. On several islands, it was impossible to walk without stepping on birds' eggs. He described how sailors dangled baited fish-hooks in the air and seized birds by the legs when they swooped down to eat the bait. He complained that the noise of the whales and porpoises in the gulf disturbed his sleep.

On shore, the French sailors traded with the Aboriginal peoples of one of the Algonquian nations, perhaps the Mi'kmaq or Montagnais. Although Champlain was surprised by their lack of clothing, their painted bodies, and their unfamiliar dances, he admired their strength, cheerfulness, intelligence, and health.

Champlain journeyed up the St. Lawrence River looking for Hochelaga, the present-day site of Montréal, but he did not find it. The Iroquois who had lived there when Cartier visited were gone. Since rapids prevented the ocean-going ships from travelling further, Champlain asked the Aboriginal peoples to tell him what lay beyond. They told him that a great lake lay ahead, followed by a waterfall, and then another lake that was so large that none had ever seen the other end. They told him the water in this lake was very salty. When Champlain returned to France later that year, he was convinced that he had found a route to Asia.

FURTHER UNDERSTANDING

Scurvy A person who lacks Vitamin C in his or her diet may develop this disease. Sailors and explorers often did not have enough fresh fruits and vegetables, which are good sources of Vitamin C. In 1604, many of the men in Champlain's settlement lost their lives to scurvy. During the difficult winter of 1535, many of Cartier's men were sick. Fortunately for them, the people of Stadacona told them about a cure. It was a drink made by boiling the bark and leaves of a cedar tree.

■ Champlain travelled to Georgian Bay by canoe in 1615. He wanted to build better relations between the French and the Huron.

The Establishment of Port-Royal

In France, Champlain told King Henry IV about his discoveries, including the plentiful supply of beaver furs. King Henry IV had already decided to start a colony in North America. He gave all the land between the 40th and 46th **parallels** of latitude to Pierre Du Gua Sieur de Monts for ten years. In return for the exclusive right to trade with the Aboriginal peoples, de Monts promised to found a colony, explore the land, and convert the Algonquians to Christianity.

De Monts hired Champlain as his cartographer, and the two became business partners. In 1604, Champlain and de Monts sailed into the Bay of Fundy with about eighty settlers. They brought supplies and goods for trading, such as knives and glass beads.

The leaders decided to stay the winter on a small island in the mouth of the Ste. Croix River. This spot was easy to defend, had hardwood trees for lumber, and sand and clay for brick making. There were many shellfish on the shore, and the soil was fertile.

It turned out they had made a poor choice. The island had no fresh water. The winter weather was severe, and the little island was soon covered by more than one metre of snow. Almost one-half of the eighty men died of scurvy and cold.

In the spring, the remaining settlers moved across the Bay of Fundy to the mainland. There, they built the colony of Port-Royal. With the help of the Mi'kmaq, who provided the settlers with food and a cure for scurvy, Port-Royal grew.

Champlain lost interest in the settlement when the king cancelled the fur trade **monopoly**. He returned to France with de Monts. While his work in New France was not over, he did not resume until 1608, when he founded a new settlement on the site of Stadacona.

■ The Order of Good Cheer was the first social club established by Europeans in North America. It was founded in 1606 by Samuel de Champlain in the settlement of Port-Royal.

Henry HUDSON

Hudson's crew mutinied and set him, his 18-year-old son, and some loyal crew members adrift in a small boat.

In 1609, another English explorer, Henry Hudson, tried to find a Northwest Passage. Hudson had already tried to sail to Asia by way of the North Pole in 1607. In 1609, he tried a different route. Hudson and his crew sailed west across the Atlantic Ocean to North America. He sailed his ship, the *Half Moon*, up a river that begins where the city of New York is today. Hudson soon realized that the river was not the Northwest Passage, and he returned to England. Today, the river is called the Hudson River.

In April 1610, Hudson and his crew set out once more to look for the Northwest Passage. This time, with Frobisher's maps to guide him, Hudson sailed northwest into the Arctic waters. After sailing through a narrow strait filled with ice, he entered a large, open body of water. He followed the coast that bordered the water. He thought he had reached the West Coast of North America. In fact, he had discovered a bay that was later named Hudson Bay.

After months of searching for a way out of the bay, and with winter fast approaching, Hudson was forced to land his ship the *Discovery*. Hudson and his crew spent the winter on shore near their boat. The weather was terrible. The sailors became ill with scurvy, and food supplies ran low.

FURTHER UNDERSTANDING

Mutiny When sailors or soldiers rebel or act against the orders of their leader, they are committing mutiny. Creating a disturbance or using violence are forms of mutiny. Taking unlawful control of a ship is another form of mutiny.

■ In his attempt to find a northern route between Europe and Asia, Henry Hudson sailed farther north than any earlier explorer.

Mutiny on the *Discovery*

As soon as the ice melted and the ship was free to sail, the crew wanted to return home. Hudson would not listen. He wanted to continue his search for the Northwest Passage.

The crew mutinied and set Hudson, his 18-year-old son, and some loyal crew members adrift in a small boat. Hudson and the others did not survive.

Although Hudson did not find the Northwest Passage, his explorations helped England lay claim to the rich fur-trading area around Hudson Bay. There were now two routes from which to transport furs from North America to Europe. The French could ship furs to France by way of the St. Lawrence River. The English could ship furs from Hudson Bay to England.

ENGLISH EXPLORERS IN THE ARCTIC

In 1612, Sir Thomas Button led an expedition along the northeast coast of North America and into northern Arctic waters. Two vessels left England: the *Resolute* and Hudson's old ship, the *Discovery*. So confident was Button that he would find the Northwest Passage to the Far East that he carried with him a personal letter from King James I addressed to the emperor of Japan. Button failed in his mission, but he was able to chart the west coast of the Hudson Bay as far as the Nelson River.

Other seafarers continued the search for the passage. While they also failed to find a Northwest Passage, they helped chart the eastern Arctic waters of the Far North. By 1650, the search for the Northwest Passage was abandoned. England's attention focussed on the settlement of North America's interior. The search did not resume until the nineteenth century, when charts and maps from these early years of exploration were put back into use. The Northwest Passage was not sailed from east to west until 1905, when Roald Amundsen from Norway finally completed the voyage.

■ The *Discovery* returned to England, but no one ever found Henry Hudson and the other people that were set adrift after the mutiny.

European Explorers in NORTH AMERICA

European Exploration of Canada
0
500
1,000 km
Scale
Cabot
Cartier
Frobisher
Champlain
Hudson
Early Settlements
N
W
E
S
Greenland
Baffin Island
FROBISHER BAY
ATLANTIC OCEAN
HUDSON BAY
Labrador
JAMES BAY
Newfoundland
GRAND BANKS
Gaspé Peninsula
Cape Brenton Island
New Brunswick
Québec
ST. LAWRENCE R.
Port-Royal
Prince Edward Island
LAKE SUPERIOR
Montréal
OTTAWA R.
LAKE CHAMPLAIN
LAKE HURON
LAKE ONTARIO
HUDSON R.
BAY OF FUNDY
Nova Scotia
LAKE MICHIGAN
LAKE ERIE
New York

The Explorers

Vikings
- Icelander Bjarni Herjulfsson saw North America when his ship blew off course
- Leif and Thorvald Eriksson, and Gudrid and Thorfun Karlsefni briefly settled in Newfoundland
- Had first contact and conflicts with Aboriginal peoples

John Cabot
- Italian explorer hired by England to find a route to the Far East
- Left on his first voyage in 1497
- Claimed Newfoundland for England
- Discovered Grand Banks fishing area

Gaspar Corte-Real
- Portuguese explorer
- Left on his first voyage 1501
- Brought Aboriginal people back to Portugal

João Alvares Fagundes
- Portuguese explorer
- First travelled to North America in 1520
- Wanted to set up a colony in Newfoundland to profit from the fishing trade in Grand Banks
- May have established a failed colony on Cape Breton Island

Giovanni da Verrazzano
- Italian explorer hired by France to find a route to the Far East
- First reached North America in 1524
- Explored the east coast of North America from Florida to Cape Breton Island
- Claimed the region for France

Jacques Cartier
- Master fisher from France who had been to the Grand Banks
- Left on his first voyage in 1534
- Explored the Gulf of St. Lawrence, visited Prince Edward Island and New Brunswick
- Claimed the land for France
- Captured Iroquois and took them back to France

Martin Frobisher
- English explorer who tried to get to Asia by sailing northwest through North America
- Left on his first voyage in 1576
- Traded and fought with the Inuit

Samuel de Champlain
- Undertook a detailed exploration of the St. Lawrence River in 1603
- Thought a route through the Great Lakes was the route to Asia
- Set up a colony at Port-Royal and later Stadacona

Henry Hudson
- English explorer who followed in Frobisher's footsteps
- Left on his first voyage in 1609
- Explored what later became Hudson Bay
- Crew mutinied against him and set him adrift at sea

The Beothuks of NEWFOUNDLAND

The Beothuks withdrew from all contact with the Europeans and went into hiding in the interior of Newfoundland.

The Beothuks lived in isolation on their island home on Newfoundland. The Beothuks' language, habits, and customs were distinct from those of the Aboriginal peoples on the mainland. They survived by fishing and hunting. In summer, they lived along the coasts. In winter, they withdrew inland.

The Beothuks walked barefoot in summer, but in winter they wore caribou skin moccasins. They wore their hair long and braided at the back of the head. They stuck feathers in their hair, usually leaving one of them sticking straight up. They lived in wigwams in winter, that were usually rectangular, but sometimes circular, in shape. Close by were their storehouses and places to smoke meat. They hunted with bows and arrows. Most of their arrowheads were made of stone or bone. They travelled in large canoes made of birch and caribou skins. Almost all of their tools were made of stone.

When the fishing trade began off Newfoundland's coast, the Europeans often encountered the Beothuks. Some Beothuks began trading furs with the newcomers, but contact was limited.

As the fishery became more established, the Europeans built drying racks, fishing sheds, and landing stages on the shores, often leaving them for the long months it took them to return to England with their catch. The Beothuks were attracted by the European goods and fishing equipment left on shore. They were used to sharing their possessions with others, so they saw nothing wrong with helping themselves to what was lying around, not being used. One day one of the fishing ships fired on them for "stealing" fishing equipment. The Beothuks withdrew from all contact with the Europeans. They went into hiding in the interior of Newfoundland.

For 200 years the Europeans and the Mi'kmaq, who came to Newfoundland from Nova Scotia, hunted the Beothuks as though they were animals. By the early 1800s, the Beothuks had been reduced to a few reclusive families. While the British government wanted to stop the murders, it was too late for the Beothuks.

■ John Guy, the governor of the first English colony in Newfoundland, is believed to have come in contact with the Beothuks in Trinity Bay.

FURTHER UNDERSTANDING

Historical record Since Shawnadithit's people had a primarily oral culture, their disappearance would have meant a disappearance of all knowledge about them. A scientist named William Epps Cormack was interested in the Beothuks and saw in Shawnadithit the last hope of learning about her people. She had learned some English and taught Cormack some of the Beothuk language. Her talent for drawing helped her tell him about her people, their history, manners, customs, and quick decline. Cormack's notes and Shawnadithit's drawings are a form of historical record.

SHAWNADITHIT: LAST OF THE BEOTHUKS

In March 1823, a group of settlers hunting fur came upon a Beothuk family. At the approach of the hunters, the family fled. The father drowned after he fell through the ice while trying to cross a creek. The mother and two daughters were exhausted from starvation. They were captured and taken to Twillingate. There, they were handed over to John Peyton, the magistrate of the district and a prominent merchant. In June, Peyton took them to St. John's, where a room was set aside for their use in the courthouse.

After a few weeks, the women were returned to the area where they had been found, bearing many gifts for their friends. They were left with a supply of food and a small boat in the hope that they would find their way back to their people. After several days of wandering, they failed to find their way back home. The three women returned to Twillingate. Soon after their return, the mother and one of the daughters died.

The other daughter, Shawnadithit, was taken into Peyton's home. She lived with the Peyton family for the next five years, helping with the household chores. Shawnadithit carved combs out of caribou horn, and decorated them with elaborate patterns. She used birch bark to produce impressions of animals or other designs. Although she kept very much to herself, she helped create a historical record of her people and their ways. In 1829, Shawnadithit died at the age of 29. She was the last of her people.

■ Shawnadithit was nearly 1.8 metres tall (5 feet, 9 inches) and was described as having handsome features.

■ Shawnadithit drew ten drawings depicting scenes in the closing history of the Beothuks. The drawings include food items, utensils, and other implements used by her people.

A Meeting of CULTURES

The Europeans did not fully understand Aboriginal languages and spiritual beliefs.

Trade between Aboriginal peoples and Europeans began slowly. At first, Europeans considered North America an obstacle to their goal—finding a route to the Far East. Later, Europeans saw the new land as a source of fish. The land itself provided a convenient supply of fresh food and water, while they filled their ships with cod.

The earliest explorers, and, later, the fishers, encountered Aboriginal groups, such as the Mi'kmaq, who lived along the eastern coasts. The Europeans learned much about the new land from them. The Mi'kmaq willingly shared their belongings and skills with the European visitors. They taught them how to use canoes, toboggans, snowshoes, and moccasins, and acted as their guides. They showed early settlers how to hunt and where to fish. When the Europeans became sick, the Aboriginal peoples showed them which roots and herbs would cure them.

Many Europeans and Aboriginal peoples were ethnocentric. Most Europeans thought that they were superior to the Aboriginal peoples because many Aboriginal peoples wore few clothes and had no firearms or metal tools. The Europeans did not fully understand Aboriginal languages and spiritual beliefs. Some Aboriginal groups considered themselves superior to the French and English due to the Europeans' inability to canoe or snowshoe very far before becoming exhausted. The Europeans' faces and bodies were covered with hair, which the Aboriginal peoples considered unattractive. While mistrust dominated many transactions, the Europeans and Aboriginal peoples had goods and information to offer each other.

The Europeans began to realize that great wealth could be made from selling furs from North America. When the fur trade began, it fit well with the Aboriginal way of life. The Aboriginal peoples had always hunted and traded for what they needed. The Aboriginal peoples liked European goods. Increasing numbers of Aboriginal peoples began to travel to the north Atlantic coast and the St. Lawrence River each summer to trade. They traded their furs for metal tools, such as knives and axes. Iron cooking pots and copper kettles replaced those made of clay, skin, bark, or wood. Guns replaced bows and arrows, and weapons made of stone and bone. Hunting for food became quicker and easier.

FURTHER UNDERSTANDING

Ethnocentric A person who believes his or her culture is superior to other cultures is ethnocentric. One cause is a misunderstanding about the other culture's values and way of life.

■ The Canadian fur trade rapidly expanded in the early 1600s due to increased demand. European beavers were dying out because of over-hunting, and beaver felt was needed for new fashions, such as hats.

Changes in Lifestyle

As the fur trade grew, Aboriginal ways of life began to change. For some groups, such as the Mi'kmaq, hunting and trapping for furs to trade replaced summer food gathering and other traditional activities. Some Aboriginal groups became more dependent on trade goods, such as clothing from Europe.

The Europeans also brought diseases, such as chicken pox, scarlet fever, smallpox, **tuberculosis**, and **whooping cough**. The Aboriginal peoples had not been exposed to these diseases before, so their bodies had no immunity to them. Even measles could be deadly. Aboriginal peoples died by the thousands from diseases.

The fur trade also changed some Aboriginal groups' way of keeping order. Instead of choosing leaders according to their wisdom, some chiefs were chosen because of their fur trading skill. As competition for the fur trade grew, so did conflicts between Aboriginal groups as they formed alliances with different European partners.

These were slow but steady changes. As more and more Europeans visited and eventually stayed in North America, the traditional ways of the Aboriginal peoples were changed forever.

■ During the fur-trade era, the Mi'kmaq served as middlemen between the French and the Aboriginal groups that lived farther west.

QUIZ (answers on page 47)

Multiple Choice
Choose the best answer in the multiple choice questions that follow.

1 Which was not one of the characteristics of the Pacific Coast potlatch?
a) At a potlatch, the host gave a gift to each one of the guests.
b) Guests were seated according to their rank.
c) Only an elite few were invited to the potlatch.
d) Chiefs and nobles gave potlatches to announce important events.

2 Which five Aboriginal groups belonged to the League of Five Nations?
a) Cayuga, Huron, Mohawk, Oneida, and Onondaga
b) Cayuga, Huron, Neutrals, Mohawk, and Onondaga
c) Neutrals, Oneida, Onondaga, Tobacco Nation, and Seneca
d) Cayuga, Mohawk, Oneida, Onondaga, and Seneca

3 What did the Viking word "Skraelings" mean?
a) Barbarians
b) Weaklings
c) Friends
d) None of the above

4 Which European explorer first discovered the Grand Banks?
a) Gaspar Corte-Real
b) Giovanni da Verrazzano
c) John Cabot
d) Jacques Cartier

5 Why did chief Donnacona lie to Francis I?
a) He thought he would be rewarded with jewels if he helped the French find the Northwest Passage.
b) He knew that the only way for him to return home was if the French went on another expedition.
c) He wanted to establish a monopoly on trade with the French.
d) Donnacona did not lie to Francis I, his stories were misunderstood.

6 Why were the Europeans first interested in North America?
a) The Europeans wanted to exploit the fishing grounds around the Grand Banks.
b) The Europeans were interested in finding a route through or around North America to the Far East.
c) The Europeans wanted to make money off the abundance of fur in North America.
d) The Europeans thought North America would be full of gold and other precious metals.

7 To whom did King Henry IV of France give exclusive trading rights in North America in the early 1600s?
a) Jacques Cartier
b) Samuel de Champlain
c) Pierre Du Gua Sieur de Monts
d) Gaspar Corte-Real

The Dawn of Canada

Mix and Match

Match the terms in column B with the correct description in column A. There are more terms than descriptions.

A

1. English explorer whose crew mutinied and set him adrift at sea
2. Type of food made from powdered meat mixed with melted fat
3. One of seven major Aboriginal groups that fished along the Northwest Coast of the Pacific Ocean
4. Sixth member of the League of Five Nations
5. Aboriginal group first encountered by Jacques Cartier on the Gaspé Peninsula
6. Italian navigator hired by France to find a route to the Far East
7. First European to sail around Africa to find a route to the spice lands of India

B

a) Tuscaroras
b) Pemmican
c) Beothuks
d) Giovanni da Verrazzano
e) Henry Hudson
f) Iroquois
g) Vasco da Gama
h) João Alvares Fagundes
i) Kwakiutl

Time Line

Find the appropriate spot on the time line for each event listed below.

A Martin Frobisher makes his first trip in search of the Northwest Passage

B Shawnadithit, last of the Beothuks, dies

C Cartier leaves North America for the last time

D Leif Eriksson, son of Erik the Red, discovers Newfoundland

E Giovanni da Verrazzano claims the eastern coast of North America for France

F Roald Amundsen completes the first voyage through the Northwest Passage

---

14,000 years ago According to some scientists, Aboriginal groups first immigrated to Alaska from Siberia

986 BC Erik the Red establishes a colony in Greenland

1001–1002 **1**

1492 Christopher Columbus discovers the Caribbean

1497 John Cabot rediscovers Newfoundland and the Grand Banks

1524 **2**

April 30, 1534 Jacques Cartier sets sail on the first of his three voyages to North America

1535–1536 Cartier spends his first winter in North America at Stadacona, the future site of Québec City

1542 **3**

1576 **4**

1570 Samuel de Champlain is born in France

1605 Champlain founds Port-Royal

1611 The crew of the *Discovery* sets Henry Hudson adrift

1829 **5**

1905 **6**

45

Conclusion

Aboriginal peoples believe that they have always lived in North America. Scientific studies have offered other explanations, such as the theory about the **Beringia** land bridge. Long before Europeans arrived in North America, Aboriginal groups had developed unique cultures that met their needs and suited their environments. Europeans stumbled upon North America when looking for quick trade routes to Asia. Monarchs, such as those in France, England, Portugal, and Spain, were willing to finance explorations to North America. They hoped to gain power and wealth from these discoveries.

Explorers who came to North America were very unfamiliar with their surroundings. They depended on Aboriginal peoples to share their knowledge and technology. Europeans began to trade pots, tools, and weapons for furs, food, and survival techniques. Contact between the two cultures also brought negative consequences, such as disease and fighting. Conflicts and competition began to increase as France and England hoped to colonize this new land.

Further Information

Suggested Reading

Cook, Ramsay (ed.). *The Voyages of Jacques Cartier.* Toronto: University of Toronto Press, 1993.

Coulter, Tony. *Jacques Cartier, Samuel de Champlain, & the Explorers of Canada.* Broomall: Chelsea House Publishers, 1993.

Dickason, Olive P. *Canada's First Nations: A History of Founding Peoples from Earliest Times.* Norman: University of Oklahoma Press, 1992.

MacDonald, George F. *Haida Art.* Seattle: University of Washington Press, 1996.

Swinton, George. *Sculpture of the Inuit.* Toronto: McClelland & Stewart, 1999.

Internet Resources

Canada: A People's History Online
history.cbc.ca
The online companion to CBC's award-winning television series on the history of Canada, as told through the eyes of its people. This multimedia Web site features behind-the-scenes information, games and puzzles, and discussion boards. It is also available in French.

The Canadian Encyclopedia Online
www.thecanadianencyclopedia.com
A reference for all things Canadian. In-depth history articles are accompanied by photographs, paintings, and maps. Articles can be read in both French and English.

Exploration, the Fur Trade, and Hudson's Bay Company
www.canadiana.org/hbc
This Web site specializes in early Canadian history. Features include a time line, stories, and personalities. Articles are available in both French and English.

Glossary

astrolabe: astronomical instrument that was once used to measure the Sun and the stars to determine location; was replaced by the sextant

awls: pointed tools used to make holes in wood and leather

Beringia: land mass that joined Siberia and Alaska during the Ice Age; now submerged

breechcloths: articles of clothing, usually made from cloth or leather, used to cover the loins; the material is passed between the legs and fastened around the waist

cached: supplies, such as food and equipment, which are hidden for future use in an area that is protected from animals and the weather

cartographer: an individual who specializes in making maps or charts

democratic: based upon the principles of democracy; government by the people

gaff: large hook attached to a pole that is used to catch fish

lean-tos: open tents with a sloped roof supported by a pole between two trees

lichens: type of plant made up of algae and fungi; typically found growing on rocks and trees

monopoly: guaranteed control of a service or market without competition; granted by the government

muskeg: type of bog or marshland made up of dead and decaying plant matter

parallels: imaginary lines that circle Earth parallel to the equator

ritual: a form of ceremony or rite performed in a place of worship

sachem: an Aboriginal leader or chief; this position is usually hereditary

sagas: stories of heroic actions; typically originating from the Vikings

sextant: astronomical instrument used to determine latitude and longitude

tuberculosis: infectious disease that causes tubercles to form in the lungs; causes extreme coughing, fever, weight loss, chest pain, and can lead to death

whooping cough: infectious disease in children characterized by coughing spasms

Answers

Multiple Choice	Mix and Match	Time Line
1. c)	1. e)	1. d)
2. d)	2. b)	2. e)
3. a)	3. i)	3. c)
4. c)	4. a)	4. a)
5. b)	5. f)	5. b)
6. b)	6. d)	6. f)
7. c)	7. g)	

Index

Algonquin 8, 9, 18, 19

Beothuk 8, 19, 22, 26, 40, 41
bison 7, 14, 15, 19

Cabot, John 26, 27, 28, 38, 39
caribou 6, 7, 12, 19, 40, 41
Cartier, Jacques 30, 31, 34, 38, 39
Champlain, Samuel de 34, 35, 38, 39
Columbus, Christopher 22, 24, 25, 26
Cree 8, 19

Dene (Chipewyans) 7, 19
Donnacona 30, 31

England 26, 28, 30, 32, 33, 36, 37, 39, 40, 46
Erik the Red 20, 21

France 29, 30, 31, 34, 35, 37, 39, 46
Frobisher, Martin 30, 32, 33, 36, 38, 39

Grand Banks 26, 27, 28, 29, 30, 38, 39
Greenland 20, 21, 22, 28, 38

Haida 10, 19
Hudson, Henry 36, 37, 38, 39
Huron 5, 16, 17, 19, 34

Interior Salish 12, 13, 19
Inuit 6, 18, 19, 32, 33, 39
Iroquois 5, 16, 17, 19, 30, 31, 34, 39

Kootenays 12, 13

L'Anse aux Meadows 22
League of Five Nations 16

Mi'kmaq 19, 30, 34, 35, 40, 42, 43
Monts, Pierre Du Gua, Sieur de 35

Northwest Passage 30, 32, 36, 37

Ojibwa 8, 9, 19

pemmican 7, 15
Port-Royal 35, 38, 39
Portugal 24, 28, 39, 46
potlatch 11, 19

Shawnadithit 40, 41
Spain 24, 25, 29, 46
St. Lawrence River 16, 30, 31, 34, 37, 38, 39, 42

teepee 8, 13, 14, 15, 19
totem pole 10, 19

Verrazzano, Giovanni da 29, 39
Vikings 20, 21, 22, 23, 26, 39
Vinland 20, 21, 22

wigwam 8, 19, 40

Yellowknives 7